Winter Roses

poems by

Hilary Sallick

Finishing Line Press
Georgetown, Kentucky

Winter Roses

In memory of Katherine Rogers
July 10, 1965 – April 14, 2013

Copyright © 2017 by Hilary Sallick
ISBN 978-1-63534-212-3 First Edition
All rights reserved under International and Pan-American Copyright Conventions.
No part of this book may be reproduced in any manner whatsoever without written permission from the publisher, except in the case of brief quotations embodied in critical articles and reviews.

ACKNOWLEDGMENTS

Thank you to my family—Bob, Will, and Verna; Mom and Da; Markie and Jol and Pia—for blessings of love and insight; and to my dear companions in poetry over the years, Lisa Schneier, Mary Buchinger, Linda Haviland Conte, and Carmi Soifer, who keep me going.

Publisher: Leah Maines

Editor: Christen Kincaid

Cover Art: Public domain, (Wikimedia) Cézanne, "Portrait of Gustave Geffroy."

Author Photo: Renato Castelo Aviles

Cover Design: Elizabeth Maines McCleavy

Printed in the USA on acid-free paper.
Order online: www.finishinglinepress.com
        also available on amazon.com

Author inquiries and mail orders:
Finishing Line Press
P. O. Box 1626
Georgetown, Kentucky 40324
U. S. A.

Table of Contents

Winter Roses 1

Yesterday in the Subway Station 2

Edna 3

Late Rain 4

Triptych 5

February 7

Observing a Man 8

Michael and Joe 9

Man with Paper Plate 11

Woman with Poem 12

Man in Public Library 13

Man at His Desk 14

Woman in Public Library 15

After Reading Chekhov 16

The View from Here 17

Coming In 18

April Life 19

The Writer in the Library 20

Spring Cleaning 21

Winter Roses

Water hums in the kettle
gathers force from flame

I wait for what will come

for hardness of truth
for softness of sky   falling

feathering   curving
the landscape

sky of motion
of churning waves invisible
sailing over the house

No dream complete on its own
I bought roses
to take me through

They stand in a glass jar
by the window   as snow
comes swirling

each rose brilliant
on its narrow stem
each thorn   needle-sharp

Yesterday in the Subway Station

As I walked down the platform to sit and wait, I saw a woman on a bench, crying.

I looked at her, without slowing my steps. She pressed silent sobs into the hard white tiles of the wall. I held her within my attention. Long yellow-brown hair fell over her face. She wore a camel-hair coat, a red plaid scarf.

When the train came, I watched her rise, wiping away tears. Her eyes held the same blank expression as everyone else's. I sat across from her, took her in with sidelong glances. Her face was young, fair-skinned, depleted. I knew her feeling. How she could let it come over her, sweep her up. So that now she was free of it.

Her stop was the same as mine, but I lost her in the crowd hurrying to the escalators. I rode up slowly, tired. I didn't push myself to use my remaining power.

Outside I followed the sidewalk of ice and snow, crossed the street. There our paths converged, and we looked at each other. Then she walked ahead along the narrow darkening way. I wonder, when I see her again, if I'll know her.

Edna

The homeless woman
passing time in this chain-store cafe
is the sister of a friend.
This is how I know
the situation she's in. Her sister
had to put her out, finally.
There are places to go at night.
There is here—a chair,
a table—where she can sit all day,
her black-and-white-checked duffel
safe on the floor beside her,
and gaze into the surface of her iPhone.

On Monday I saw her in the art museum,
alone in a doorway,
dazed and leaning. Peaceful
throngs stood in line for Goya. Children at long tables
decorated construction-paper crowns to celebrate
the legacy of Dr. Martin Luther King
for it was Monday, January 19, 2015.
Admission was free,
and Edna, resourceful,
lived there for the day.

She chews gum slowly, her being
wiped clean. Beyond the wide plate-glass,
pigeons flash. She bothers no one.
This is what she would tell her sister.
She wasn't in the way. She didn't take
anything. She cooked sometimes. (She is
a good cook, everyone agrees.)

It's dusk outside.
Long shadows stripe the plaza,
long strokes of orange as the glowing sun
sinks. A little child passes by,
arm up-stretched to hold
her father's hand.

Late Rain

From above a hawk swoops down
wide black wings   then
orange leaves in the woods
mostly branches   sticks   gray-green lichens
stems of trunks that wind upward
into twigs   squirrels' nests   winter sky

Now raindrops take their forms
come falling
to puddles   tops of cars   stems of grasses
to petals   the oily backs
of waterbirds

Other birds find shelter   between trunk
and branch of deep spruce   in crevice
of rock   as I too
wait it out   imagine dampening trickling
wings

Each droplet falls alone   rejoins
the pond   the flowing rivulet
I hear the singular notes   dripping
drumming   low
and high   as one becomes many
is lost in the memory
of the larger one

Triptych

1. In the Museum

Face to face with Goya's passionate naked
youth   who wistful on rock in desert raises
the delicate banner   *Ecce Agnus Dei*
I find myself   full of feeling   of failure   of
desire   missed chances

In the museum's crowded hush
the sharpness of longing
rises without purpose

2. In the City Park

He sits motionless
in the cold
on a round concrete pedestal
one of sixteen
in a perfect circle
with four square tables
bearing checkerboard
centers
He is the only living person
there
hunched
in a winter coat

Now he smokes a cigarette
Now the gray clouds release
a few frozen particles of
stinging ice
No one is looking for him
He is free

Even the pigeons are absent today
The leafless trees have not begun
to generate new cells
but wait   wait

3. In the Kitchen

The floor calls me
to lay myself upon it
hip limb bone
on winter-cold boards
body held up
by the ungiving
surface   The floor
calls me down
to lay myself long
on the fact of it
the hard
truth
the inevitability of body
held up
sinking down
the necessary
ground

February

month of potential   a shovel   a plow   a mass of snow
parted   then more   snow on snow

I make my way along the road   between the rises of ice   the
frozen layers   the tumbling of delicate crystals

I walk freely over white crisp pathways   falling snow of blue light
of shadow and curve more than I can say

I don't stop to look for words in the sharp
blowing air   I keep going

Observing a Man

He holds the sticky almond-sliver-coated bun, raises it to his mouth, without a glint of pleasure. His bespectacled eyes look nowhere. He wears a winter parka, a gold wedding band. Once he was a child. Now he sits slumped, tilted, with crossed legs. Utterly alone.

The almond bun finished, he procures from the jumble of wrappers before him a large blueberry muffin, methodically devours it. A glass bottle of papaya juice waits, its blue lid tightly sealed. He shakes the bottle, pops the lid.

Now I pause in my observations, consider the voices in my head, the arguments and questions, the dreams and worries. My phone lights up. I speak to Lisa as he rises, clutching iPad and folded cane (*for seeing*, I realize). He deposits the wrappers in the trash, with a side to side effort makes his way out of my frame of vision. Lisa has said goodbye. I am alone with myself, my voices, my navigations through this world, the real imagined world.

Michael and Joe

The men in worn-out clothes that hang from their worn-out bodies step out to smoke, lean on a post, in shaggy pants, shuffled shoes. Unshaven, unwashed, cheerful. A life of the moment. Bent in the clouds of their smoke. What comes is released, not held, not turned over and over. Their conversation, soundless through the glass, passes back and forth.

Then they come back into the coffee shop, encounter a woman who's sure she knows the one named Michael from somewhere. Maybe in Seattle twenty-five years ago? They did something big together, but she can't quite remember. Has he ever taught yoga? Meditation? She gives them a mozzarella panini, says her eyes are bigger than her stomach. Talks about her job. Massage for stress reduction, $85 an hour. A really nice place. You should come in. Her voice innocent, wide open. Michael laughs while sipping his coffee. Then has a coughing fit that goes on and on. The massage therapist is perturbed, soothing. You gotta laugh, she coos as he recovers.

A weird day, Michael says to Joe after she has left. First I run into you here. Then I meet this girl I've never seen before who thinks she knows me. Then I almost die from choking. I think she wants me. But I don't need the complication. He rises, offers Joe a ride to his place, but no, Joe has other plans.

Michael lumbers out the door. Joe, hunched at the table, is alone now, in his brown knit cap. His worn-out face. After a bit, he goes to the window, leans on the high counter. His right foot has fallen asleep. He keeps both feet moving for some seconds, his being made of thought and pain. Steam rises from the cups of the young women at the next table. They sit face to face, every strand of hair shines, polished red nails gesture. His table beside theirs holds his belongings, bags within bags, the contents tightly bound.

Now he's getting ready to leave. First he wraps his face against the cold. Then a blanket, thin, shawl-like, over head and shoulders. His gray pillow and black sack secure in his arms. He steps out into the waiting world.

Man with Paper Plate

Once I saw a man completely engrossed, writing on a paper plate. I tried, by discreet sideways glances, to categorize his project. I saw columns of small black symbols, blocks of tight lines neatly arranged over the round face. He was alone, from another era, immaculate in coat and tie (it might even have been a bow tie). I almost asked him what he was doing, then thought better of it. It was a rigid white plate—not some last-resort flimsy scrap—as if he'd come prepared to work on that very material, cardboard with a bit of soft texture that must have been substantive, satisfying to the touch. He sat away from the windows, in the warm center of the room beside the brightly lit, glassed-in croissants. I, too, was alone at a table, making marks with a black pen, strangers milling all around. No one could touch the field of his attention. Steadily, he gazed into the receptive surface, scratching now and then more inscrutable, brilliant lines there.

Woman with Poem

Aware that everyone must be looking at her, she steps slowly through space in flowing garments (tattered and dirt-soaked at the hem), filling her coffee cup, going back for more sugar. My eyes are drawn to her.

She wears dark purple, draped by green, bracelets, necklaces. Black hair sways past her shoulders, her eyes are smudged with mascara.

Seated with a companion, she discusses a financial opportunity. She takes nothing for granted, won't be fooled again, she promises him, though the numbers do sound good. They sound too good. She bends over her bag, seeking a relevant poem.

The orange bag is crammed full, its rectangular form revealed, expanded to the utmost. Edges and surfaces of papers, grimy and bent, protrude unevenly, necessary, awaiting her touch.

Man in Public Library

Enclosed, his back to the world, he types all morning into his laptop, claiming the keys at high speed. When a worker (her blouse of shiny blue stretched over her pregnant belly) wheels the cart into his aisle, he freezes. She's behind him to his right, reaching to shelve *Emerson's Collected Writings*. She must have brushed him, barely connected her sleeve to his, for his voice startles the room's silence: *Don't touch me! Leave me alone!* She backs away, wordless. He burrows in deeper, keeps on typing, each moment protected. A wool cap shields his shaved head, the dark-green down coat, precisely belted, shelters his back, the bag on the floor beside him, zippered, immaculate, contains his life. Across the room now, she works in History, feels the baby stirring within her.

Man at His Desk
Portrait of Gustave Geffroy, Cézanne, 1895

He has brought himself here, to a work he despairs of finishing. Scattered before him: four open books, off-kilter, luminous on the darker surface. A rose leans from an orb-shaped vase. A statuette of a woman, hand on hip, observes the scene skeptically, her figure bisected by the edge of the canvas.

His vision blurs. He's looking beyond, unconscious of words upon words, the shelves of volumes framing his head. More than brushstrokes and paint the artist painstakingly works for months, his gaze continues, unfinished. The room grows cold without a fire.

Buttoned into his dark wool jacket, immobile on solid angles of elbows, he forgets the pen, fallen, somewhere, from his loose right hand. Now both hands are objects. Placed on the table with the books, they curve as if to hold something, as if with readiness, futility. A petal may be about to fall from the rose. He may be about to find the language he needs.

Eventually, the artist comes and goes for the last time.

Woman in Public Library

The woman across the way
is studying   line by line
preparing herself

Quiet surrounds us

Her bright white cuffs
emerge from dark sleeves
the window a halo behind her

Something large is at stake
a future   a credential

She holds a yellow pencil
puts trust in each page

Time passes

From within my carrel
of purple felt-tip-scrawled wood
and messages of love

I hold her

After Reading Chekhov

I considered knocking, then decided against it. Because I had no invitation, no explanation for my presence. Nothing more than my own desire. So I opened the door myself, entered the house. Paintings on the walls. A grand piano. Comfortable places to sit. My feeling of being drawn in expanded. Here was a life. I was looking around, just starting to see where I was, when a woman appeared. She regarded me with polite amazement. I began apologizing; there was nothing I could say. The man of the house walked over just then, the draft of a story in his hands. They were clearly in the middle of things, going about their day. I remembered the fact of some mutual friends and tried to make the connection, but they were discussing other matters in Russian. I was already forgotten. Still, I wanted something—to be noticed, to become necessary. Then I was alone, walking down the path away from their house, back into the rest of the world.

The View from Here

Light is returning.
Here in the café the regulars
discuss the forecast, the new baby,
when the city will plow the roads.
The simple one, aging and innocent,
who passes his days in this public space
is greeting his friend.
Whatchadoin'! How's Uncle Bobby?
Sidewalks nice and clean?
They go way back, almost brothers.
The Tibetan waitress pausing by their table
is smiling, warm and lovely,
with her curly dark ponytail,
her gold and topaz ring.
In the distance the wind tosses a flag,
buffets the rectangle of cloth back and forth,
the parallel stripes bending, curling.
The flag almost disappears behind the pole
when you look from here.

Coming In

She adjusts her red felt hat   soft
bowl atop her head   then comes
through the glass doors   black purse
hanging from the crook of her arm
She moves with small tentative
steps   looks about with meek
curiosity   What is here for her?
She peers at trays of pastries   reaching
for nothing   then selects a spot
to perch   Yes she is birdlike
behind her glasses   with a bright gaze
Seated   she's digging into the
black purse   She counts the
dollars arrayed in her hands
the hand she's been dealt
She holds a pen   bends to
write a note   Her red hat
bobs above the table

April Life

The branches are tossing their prickly baubles
swinging them on little stems.
Now and then white feathery seeds appear
blown this way and that.

A man with nowhere to go
leans—half-standing, half-sitting
against a concrete table,
hands stuffed in pockets, shoulders hunched.
The ends of the reddening branches dance.
Last year's leaves tumble by.
There's a dash of wings. A sparrow
lands briefly. But a robin stays,
erect, stock-still, then
hops (with barest vertical motion)
a short straight path,
jabs its beak into earth, repeats.

And the man has begun arguing into his phone
in the uncomfortable cold light
on the hard cold furniture.
Someone is not listening to him.
He must be louder.
There is something he desperately
needs.

The Writer in the Library

A woman   manuscript in hand
paces the mezzanine   silently reading
the pages she holds

Her mind
like a brook at the end of winter
is making a path

each step a thought
a motion into thought

Sections of melting snow
break off suddenly

She circles   past dozers
and internet-searchers
past time-passers   whisperers
over gray soundless
carpet

Water flows   fast or slow
outlasting what contains it
I hear her soft step
passing

Spring Cleaning

I hold the pen
draw lines and words

the branches of the mulberry
where squirrels run their roads through blue sky
the window into my neighbor's kitchen
where he's painting the walls and cupboards
his table piled high with dishes   teakettle
roller and paint tray

I dreamed in the night that I
was organizing my life   finally
getting on with it
There were skis   suitcases   multiple
vacuum cleaners   I was
freeing up wide spaces

Icicles   suspended from the
neighbor's roof   drip
in the warming air   narrower and
narrower   running down in bright
droplets   falling
to the garden

Now a whole chunk   just separated
broke away   vanished!

Hilary Sallick, a poet and educator, lives and works in Somerville, MA, where she and her husband raised their two children. Her poems have appeared in anthologies and journals, including *Birdsong* (FootHills Publishing), *Passager, The Human Journal, the Aurorean, Third Wednesday, Salamander,* and *the Atlanta Review*. She is an adult literacy teacher and vice-president of the New England Poetry Club. Her deep interest in learning and teaching animates all her work.

www.ingramcontent.com/pod-product-compliance
Lightning Source LLC
LaVergne TN
LVHW041525070426
835507LV00013B/1818